THE
Miracles
OF JESUS

PARTICIPANT'S GUIDE

The Deeper Connections Series

The Miracles of Jesus

The Last Days of Jesus

The Forgiveness of Jesus

The Life of Jesus

Contents

We all know Christians who are bored with Bible study—not because the Bible is boring, but because they haven't been introduced to its meaning in its first-century context and how that is significant for our lives today. When we begin to understand some of these "deeper connections"—both to the first century and to the twenty-first century—our lives are transformed.

The idea for the Deeper Connections series grew out of a concern that far too many Bible studies lack depth and solid biblical application. We wanted a Bible study series that was written and taught by biblical experts who could also communicate that material in a *clear, practical, understandable* manner. The Deeper Connections teachers have one foot in the historical, biblical text and the other in the modern world; they not only have written numerous books, they have many years of pastoral experience. When they teach in the local church, they often hear, "Wow, I've never heard it explained that way before." Unfortunately that's because, until recently, Bible professors usually spent most of their time writing books for other professors or occasionally for pastors, and the layperson in the church had little access to this biblical knowledge. Deeper Connections seeks to remedy this by bringing the best in biblical scholarship directly to small groups and Sunday school classes through the popular medium of DVD.

Don't be scared by the word "deeper"—deeper does not mean that these studies are hard to understand. It simply means that we are attempting to get at the true meaning of the biblical text, which involves investigating the historical, religious, and social background of first-century Jewish culture and their Greek and Roman neighbors. If we fail to study and understand this background, then we also fail to understand the deeper and true meaning of the Bible.

After making deeper connections to the biblical texts, the teachers then apply that text to life in the twenty-first century. This is where a deeper look into the text really pays off. Life-application in the church today has sometimes been a bit shallow and many times unrelated to the biblical passage itself. In this series, the practical application derives directly out of the biblical text.

So, to borrow the alternate title of *The Hobbit*, J. R. R. Tolkien's bestselling classic, we invite you to join us on an adventure to "there and back again"! Your life won't be the same as a result.

Deeper CONNECTIONS

THE
Miracles
OF JESUS
PARTICIPANT'S GUIDE

Six In-depth Studies Connecting the Bible to Life

Matt Williams
General Editor

 HENDRICKSON PUBLISHERS   ROSE PUBLISHING

Deeper Connections:
The Miracles of Jesus Participant's Guide
© 2007, 2016 Matt Williams
Rose Publishing, LLC
P.O. Box 3473
Peabody, Massachusetts 01961-3473 USA
Email: info@hendricksonrose.com
www.hendricksonrose.com

Cover Design: Jeff Gifford
Cover Photo: Masterfile
Interior Design: Mark Sheeres

Printed in the United States of America
December 2017, 4th printing

About the Video Teachers

Dr. Gary Burge is professor of New Testament at Wheaton College in Wheaton, Illinois, and a sought-after conference speaker. His experiences in Beirut, Lebanon, in the early 1970s when civil war broke out have helped him to see how valuable it is to understand the world of the Middle East in order to correctly understand the biblical world of Jesus. Gary is the author of many books, including a commentary on the gospel of John.

Dr. David Garland is professor of Christian Scriptures at Truett Theological Seminary, Baylor University, Waco, Texas. David is closely connected to local church ministry and has served as interim pastor of fifteen churches in Kentucky, Indiana, and Texas. He is author of many books, including commentaries on the gospels of Matthew and Mark.

Dr. Mark Strauss is professor of New Testament at Bethel Seminary in San Diego, California. He is a frequent preacher at San Diego area churches and has served in three interim pastorates. Mark is the author of many books, including a commentary on the gospel of Luke and *Four Portraits, One Jesus: An Introduction to Jesus and the Gospels.*

Dr. Michael Wilkins is professor of New Testament Language and Literature and the dean of the faculty at Talbot School of Theology, Biola University, La Mirada, California. Michael speaks throughout the world about his two passions: surfing and discipleship. He was senior pastor of two different churches in California and has written numerous books, including two commentaries on the gospel of Matthew.

Dr. Matt Williams is associate professor of New Testament at Talbot School of Theology, Biola University, La Mirada, California. A former missionary to Spain, Matt preaches and teaches at churches throughout the United States and Spain. He is general editor of *Colección Teológica Contemporánea*, a series of theological books in Spanish, and is the author of two books on the Gospels.

Dr. Ben Witherington III is professor of New Testament at Asbury Theological Seminary in Wilmore, Kentucky. Ben is an avid fan of jazz and sports, especially the Atlanta Braves. He has led numerous study tours through the lands of the Bible and is known for bringing the text to life through incisive historical and cultural analysis. He is a prolific author, including commentaries on all four gospels.

Host **Jarrett Stevens** is director of the college and singles ministry and teacher for 7/22 at North Point Church in Alpharetta, Georgia. Prior to that he was on staff at Willow Creek Community Church in suburban Chicago.

The Clean Daughter

A Bleeding Woman
(Mark 5:21–34)

Dr. Gary Burge

"Daughter, your faith has healed you. Go in peace and be freed from your suffering."

Mark 5:34

Twelve years of shame and frustration are resolved in a momentary touch of Jesus.

James Edwards

INTRODUCTION

Video Opener

Scripture Reading: Mark 5:21–34, followed by a prayer that God will open your heart as you study his Word

Location of Miracle: Near Capernaum, northwest edge of the Sea of Galilee

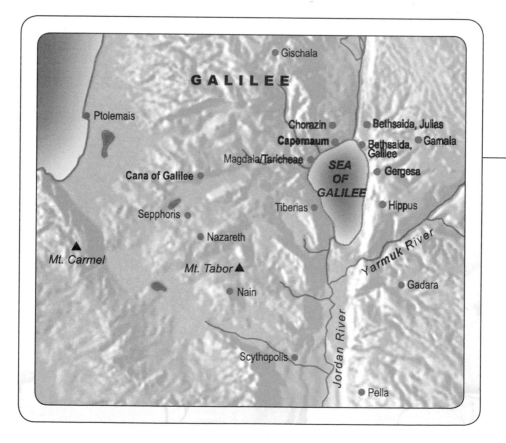

CONNECTING TO THE BIBLE

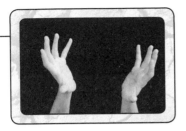

Jesus was often impressed with people who took enormous risks to find him and reach for his grace: Samaritans, lepers, the poor, women ...

Video Teaching #1 Notes

Location of Video Teaching: Hope House in Chicago's Lawndale neighborhood

Jesus looked for those on the outskirts of society

Jairus pleads with Jesus to heal his daughter

DID YOU KNOW?

Synagogue rulers were elected positions of esteem. They had responsibilities for arranging the synagogue services and overseeing the building.

Robert Guelich

Then one of the synagogue rulers, named Jairus, came there. Seeing Jesus, he fell at his feet and pleaded earnestly with him, "My little daughter is dying. Please come and putyour hands on her so that she will be healed and live." So Jesus went with him.

Mark 5:22–24

Jesus is interrupted by another daughter

The nature of her disease

> And a woman was there who had been subject to bleeding for twelve years. She had suffered a great deal under the care of many doctors and had spent all she had, yet instead of getting better she grew worse.
>
> Mark 5:25–26

DID YOU KNOW?

One remedy doctors used consisted of a dose of Persian onions cooked in wine and administered with the summons, "Arise out of your flow of blood."

Willliam Lane

When the woman touches Jesus, suddenly the entire street scene changes

> When she heard about Jesus, she came up behind him in the crowd and touched his cloak, because she thought, "If I just touch his clothes, I will be healed." Immediately her bleeding stopped and she felt in her body that she was freed from her suffering.
>
> Mark 5:27–29

The woman risks passing her unclean condition to Jesus

Has Jairus lost his chance to receive Jesus' help?

VIDEO DISCUSSION #1

1. Looking back at the Bible passage and your video teaching notes, what did you learn that you did not know previously? Consider specifically:

    • The woman who was bleeding

    • The risk that she was taking

    • The vast social difference between this woman and Jairus's daughter

    • The difference between unclean and clean in Jewish society

    • The disappointment that Jairus must have felt

    How does this knowledge help you to understand the miracle better?

2. Gary Burge said, "What's exciting about this story is that whenever Jesus has contact with people like this, he doesn't pause a moment. Jesus stops the parade because Jesus wants contact with a woman such as this." Why do you think Jesus wants contact with such people?

3. Have there been times when you have felt unclean or unworthy to go to God with your problems? What did you do?

GOING DEEPER

Because we live in the twenty-first century, it is impossible for us to understand some of the cultural, historical, and religious backgrounds of what was happening in this Mark 5 street scene. Let's investigate these details.

Video Teaching #2 Notes

The bleeding condition causes problems

Legal consequences

Social and religious consequences

Greco-Roman superstitions

> Contact with the monthly "flow" of women turns new wine sour, makes crops wither, kills skin grafts, dries seeds in gardens, causes the fruit of trees to fall off, dims the bright surface of mirrors, dulls the edge of steel and the gleam of ivory, kills bees, rusts iron and bronze.... Dogs who come near become mad and their bite becomes poisonous. A thread from an infected dress is sufficient to do all of this. If linen that is being washed and boiled is touched by such a woman, it will turn black. Such a woman has magic power—she can drive away hailstorms and whirlwinds if she shows herself when lightning flashes.
>
> Pliny the Elder, ancient Roman historian

What can we assume about this woman's life?

Her discharge of blood causes her to be discharged from society.

David Garland

Jewish garments

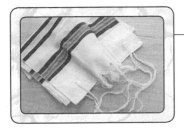

The symbolism of tassels

The LORD said to Moses, "Speak to the Israelites and say to them: 'Throughout the generations to come you are to make tassels on the corners of your garments, with a blue cord on each tassel. You will have these tassels to look at and so you will remember all the commands of the LORD.

Numbers 15:37–39

The woman reaches for the tassels of Jesus' garment

Tassel-wearing Jewish man at Jerusalem's Western Wall

Just then a woman who had been subject to bleeding for twelve years came up behind him and touched the edge of his cloak. She said to herself, "If I only touch his cloak, I will be healed."

Matthew 9:20–21

What a difference there is between the crowds that are curious about Jesus and the few who reach out and touch him!

Mark Fackler

The response of Jesus to the woman's touch

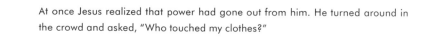

At once Jesus realized that power had gone out from him. He turned around in the crowd and asked, "Who touched my clothes?"

Mark 5:30

Jesus speaks of "your faith"; it is important that the woman understand that she had not been cured by magic ... her cure had been the result of a mighty power in Jesus, but it came to her because of her faith, not because of magic in a touch.

Leon Morris

VIDEO DISCUSSION #2

1. What do you think it was like for this woman to live in her village for twelve years with a bleeding condition (Mark 5:25–26), both religiously and socially?

   Have you ever been in a situation where you felt like an outcast? Briefly describe it, if you would like.

2. What do you think is the full meaning of what the woman was communicating to Jesus by reaching for the fringe of his garment (Mark 5:27–29, 34)?

3. Why do you think Jesus responded to her?

CONNECTING THE BIBLE TO LIFE

Jesus is approached in a Galilean village by Jairus, the leader of the synagogue, whose daughter is sick. When Jesus begins to move toward his home, the parade is stopped by the unexpected interruption of a woman who has been sick for twelve years.

Video Teaching #3 Notes

Who in our society is like this woman today?

No criticism or judgment from Jesus

> "Daughter, your faith has healed you. Go in peace and be freed from your suffering."
>
> Mark 5:34

The word translated "healed" is literally "saved." Both physical healing and theological salvation are in mind.

W. W. Wessel

Jesus, the only rabbi with the capacity to make the unclean clean

DID YOU KNOW?

No one else in the Gospels is addressed by Jesus as "daughter."

R. T. France

It was the *grasp of her faith* rather than her hand that had secured the healing she sought.

William Lane

In God's kingdom the nobodies become somebodies.

David Garland

VIDEO DISCUSSION #3

1. What is it about this woman's behavior — behavior that is commended by Jesus — that ought to be a part of our lives today?

2. Gary Burge talked about the difficulty of bringing some of the men from Hope House to his own church because of societal judgments. Are there people in your life that you might see as "unclean" who need to encounter Jesus, the powerful one? How might you be able to reach them for Jesus?

3. What would our churches have to do in order to begin embracing the homeless, drug addicts, and AIDs patients?

MAKING DEEPER CONNECTIONS IN YOUR OWN LIFE

Personal reflection studies to do on your own

Day One

1. Read Mark's gospel, chapters 4 and 5.

2. Who is Jesus? In the broader context of Mark 4–5, what miracles does Jesus perform? How do these miracles of power work together to show us who Jesus is?

3. After you have looked at the broader context of Mark 4–5 and seen how different people react to what Jesus does for them, reflect on how you have responded to this powerful Messiah.

Day Two

1. Read Mark 5:27–30.

2. What would it look like today to go to Jesus with abandon and with risk, as this woman did (Mark 5:27)? Would you consider that you yourself have gone to Jesus with abandon? Or with hesitation?

3. Though Jesus is the powerful one, he also took time to help a bleeding woman. How do we use our power — our positions in business or society, our money, our influence — to help people today? Do we use our power to promote self, or do we use it to help others, even the most unfortunate of society?

Day Three

1. Read Matthew 9:18–22, noting the similarities to and differences from Mark 5:21–34.

2. Certainly every society has people who are excluded like the woman in this passage. Who would qualify in your community? How does the average person treat them? How do conservative religious people treat them? Reflect on how Jesus might treat them.

3. Jesus addressed this woman who was an outcast of society for twelve years as "daughter" (Mark 5:34). Self-image problems plague us today. How does the fact that *you* are a "daughter" or "son" of the Creator of the world influence your own self-image and identity?

Day Four

1. Read Luke 8:40–48, noting the similarities to and differences from Mark 5:21–34.

2. Jesus brought healing to every facet of this woman's life—physical, social, emotional, and spiritual—evidenced especially by his words "Go in peace" (Mark 5:34), from the Hebrew *shalom*, signifying wholeness. How are you ministering to people in your life? Is *your* ministry a "whole"-istic ministry? In other words, do you focus on the whole person, or just on physical needs to overcome physical poverty, or just on spiritual needs to overcome spiritual poverty?

3. Though the bleeding woman was healed (Mark 5:28, 34), she would experience other physical problems in the future and eventually she would die. How do you think her experience recorded here helped her face subsequent trials?

4. Reflect on the nature of miracles today. Why do you think that God does not always answer prayer with a miracle? When he does not, does that mean that we do not have enough faith? In such circumstances, how can we maintain hope like Martin Luther, who said as they nailed his daughter's coffin closed, "Hammer away! On doomsday she'll rise again"?

Day Five

1. Read Mark 5:21–34 one more time.

2. Pray through this entire passage verse by verse, allowing the deeper meaning you have discovered to lead you as you pray. Ask the Spirit to continue to remind you of what you have learned and to help you apply these truths to your life.

3. Turn back to the discussion questions from the video teaching (Video Discussion #1, #2, #3). If there are questions that your group did not have time to discuss or questions that you might like to think more about, use this time to review and reflect further.

The Heartbeat of God

Water to Wine
(John 2:1–11)

Dr. Matt Williams

"Everyone brings out the choice wine first and then the cheaper wine after the guests have had too much to drink; but you have saved the best till now."

❧ John 2:10

I like the comparison of John's gospel to a pool in which a child may wade and an elephant can swim. It is both simple and profound.

❧ Leon Morris

INTRODUCTION

Video Opener

Scripture Reading: John 2:1–11, followed by a prayer that God will open your heart as you study his Word

Location of Miracle: Cana of Galilee. According to D. A. Carson, the most likely site is Khirbet Qana, an uninhabited ruin nine miles north of Nazareth.

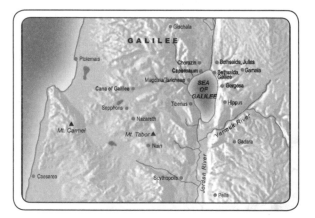

Khirbet Qana

CONNECTING TO THE BIBLE

Behind this apparently simple miracle we find deep theological significance. The water-to-wine miracle is more than a miracle, it shows us exactly who Jesus is and why he came to earth.

Video Teaching #1 Notes

Location of Video Teaching: Temecula, California

Jesus was attending a wedding

DID YOU KNOW?

Weddings in those days might have lasted up to a full week. (See the account of Samson's marriage to the young Philistine woman in Judges 14, particularly verse 12.)

On the third day a wedding took place at Cana in Galiliee.

John 2:1

Some think that Mary expected a miracle

Jesus' mother said to him, "They have no more wine." "Dear woman, why do you involve me?" Jesus replied. "My time has not yet come." His mother said to the servants, "Do whatever he tells you."

John 2:3–5

Jesus was thirty years old and had never performed a miracle

Stone water jars

> Nearby stood six stone water jars, the kind used by the Jews for ceremonial
> washing, each holding from twenty to thirty gallons.
>
> John 2:6
>
> ———————————————— ⊙ ————————————————
>
> The Pharisees and all the Jews do not eat unless they give their hands a ceremonial
> washing.
>
> Mark 7:3

Jars found in Ekron

The amount of water

Jesus said to the servants, "Fill the jars with water"; so they filled them to the brim.

John 2:7

The quality of the wine

DID YOU KNOW?

Wine in the ancient world was diluted with water to between one-third and one-tenth of its fermented strength.

D. A. Carson

The master of the banquet tasted the water that had been turned into wine.... Then he called the bridegroom aside and said, " ... You have saved the best till now."

John 2:9–10

The disciples "put their faith in" or "believed in" Jesus

This, the first of his miraculous signs, Jesus performed at Cana in Galilee. He thus revealed his glory, and his disciples put their faith in him.

John 2:11

Those who believe in Jesus become his possession. As a result of believing in Jesus, there should be a total difference in the way we live, in how we use our money, in how we think, in the TV shows that we watch, in how we treat our families, in how we spend our free time. Believing in Jesus changes everything.

Matt Williams

VIDEO DISCUSSION #1

1. Looking back at the Bible passage and your video teaching notes, what did you learn that you did not know previously? Consider specifically:

   • The meaning of the phrase "put their faith in"

   • The removal of shame from the family

   • The large quantity of wine

   • Jewish cleansing practices

   How does this knowledge help you to understand the miracle better?

2. What changes have you seen in your life since you first "believed in" Jesus that show that you are his possession?

3. Why do you think that there is a tendency for people to say that they "believe in Jesus" even though their lives do not show any real difference from the larger culture? What could be done to change this?

GOING DEEPER

Perhaps the most important aspect of determining the meaning of this miracle for the Jews of the first century is to understand Old Testament prophecies.

Video Teaching #2 Notes

The significance of a wedding

Jesus spoke to them again in parables, saying, "The kingdom of heaven is like a king who prepared a wedding banquet for his son."

Matthew 22:1–2

As a bridegroom rejoices over his bride, so will your God rejoice over you.

Isaiah 62:5

The significance of wine

Isaiah 25: A picture of kingdom plenty

> On this mountain the LORD Almighty will prepare a feast of rich food for all peoples, a banquet of aged wine—the best of meats and the finest of wines.
>
> Isaiah 25:6

The picture of the kingdom of God as a feast is prominent in Judaism and in the synoptic teaching, and the abundance of wine is a feature of the feast.

George Beasley-Murray

Jeremiah 31: The sign of a new covenant

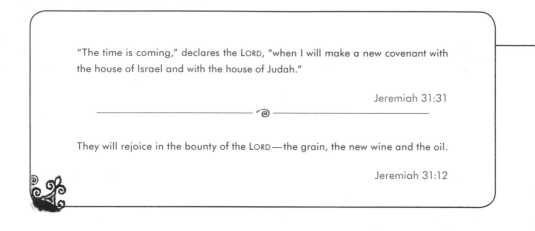

"The time is coming," declares the LORD, "when I will make a new covenant with the house of Israel and with the house of Judah."

Jeremiah 31:31

They will rejoice in the bounty of the LORD—the grain, the new wine and the oil.

Jeremiah 31:12

Jewish rabbis taught that becoming drunk was not acceptable. That drunkenness is part of the celebration at Cana is unlikely. See also Ephesians 5:18.

Craig Keener

Amos 9: The restoration of the Davidic kingship

"In that day I will restore David's fallen tent. I will repair its broken places, restore its ruins, and build it as it used to be.... New wine will drip from the mountains and flow from all the hills."

Amos 9:11, 13

The earth will yield fruits ten thousandfold. And on each vine there will be a thousand branches, and each branch will produce a thousand clusters, and each cluster will produce a thousand grapes, and each grape will produce one hundred and twenty gallons of wine.

2 Baruch 29:5

This miracle is not about drinking wine or getting drunk; it is about the fulfillment of Old Testament prophecies about the coming new covenant and its accompanying sign, wine. While drinking wine was a normal custom in the Jewish culture, it was very clear that drunkenness was not acceptable: "Woe to those who rise early in the morning to run after their drinks, who stay up late at night till they are inflamed with wine" (Isaiah 5:11).

Matt Williams

Summary of Jewish expectations

The abundant provision at these shared meals is symbolic of the joy of God's uncalculating forgiveness, and a pointer to the eschatological messianic banquet.

Craig Blomberg

The deeper meaning of Jesus changing water to wine

The mention of the Jewish purification water jars makes clear that the author [John] wishes to suggest that Jesus replaces the rituals and institutions of early Judaism with something more life-giving and enduring.

Ben Witherington III

But the ministry Jesus has received is as superior to theirs as the covenant of which he is mediator is superior to the old one, and it is founded on better promises....
"The time is coming, declares the Lord, when I will make a new covenant with the house of Israel and with the house of Judah."

Hebrews 8:6, 8

The new covenant is in no way anti-Jewish. Rather, it is inclusive. It includes all Jews and Gentiles who repent and receive the long-awaited Messiah.

Matt Williams

Result: The disciples believe in Jesus

Jesus is the Messiah, the Son of David, who comes to fulfill Judaism and bring the expected kingdom of God.

Matt Williams

VIDEO DISCUSSION #2

1. Given the Old Testament prophecies in Isaiah 25, Jeremiah 31, and Amos 9, do you think that the Jewish people at the wedding in Cana would have understood this miracle of turning water to wine? Why or why not?

2. The ending of this miracle shows us that the disciples *did* understand the significance of this miracle: "He thus revealed his glory, and his disciples put their faith in him" (John 2:11). But I wonder if *we* in the twenty-first century fully understand it. What do you think is the full meaning and significance of Jesus turning the water into wine? (Don't forget the significance of the water which was in the jars before the wine.) Use your own words to explain the meaning of the passage to those in your group.

3. The master of the banquet said that this wine was the "best." How is the new covenant "superior to" the old covenant? See Hebrews 8.

CONNECTING THE BIBLE TO LIFE

When we understand that Jesus' mission was to be a blessing to the entire world—as John 3:16 says, "For God so loved the world"—can our own mission be any different?

Video Teaching #3 Notes

Jesus takes away our shame

> If we confess our sins, he is faithful and just and will forgive us our sins and purify us from all unrighteousness.
>
> 1 John 1:9

God is faithful

> Know therefore that the LORD your God is God; he is the faithful God, keeping his covenant of love to a thousand generations of those who love him and keep his commands.
>
> Deuteronomy 7:9

A common theme

On this mountain the LORD Almighty will prepare a feast of rich food for all peoples, a banquet of aged wine.

Isaiah 25:6

———————————— ◎ ————————————

Hear the word of the LORD, O nations; proclaim it in distant coastlands: "He who scattered Israel will gather them and will watch over his flock like a shepherd."

Jeremiah 31:10

———————————— ◎ ————————————

"So that they may possess the remnant of Edom and all the nations that bear my name," declares the LORD, who will do these things.

Amos 9:12

Reaching the nations is not a new idea

> "I will bless those who bless you, and whoever curses you I will curse; and all peoples on earth will be blessed through you."
>
> Genesis 12:3

Our mission: reach the nations

VIDEO DISCUSSION #3

1. In the same way that the Jewish people of the first century
   sometimes forgot about the nations, the church today
   sometimes forgets the importance of being a blessing to the
   nations. What would we do differently, both as individuals
   and as churches, if we really grasped that our mission is to
   be a blessing to "all nations," starting in our communities and
   moving to the entire world?

2. In what ways has God taken away our shame? What has helped
   you to accept his grace and forgiveness in your life?

3. God showed his faithfulness in sending Jesus to fulfill Old
   Testament prophecies. How has God shown his faithfulness to
   you in the past few months?

MAKING DEEPER CONNECTIONS IN YOUR OWN LIFE

Personal reflection studies to do on your own

Day One

1. Read Deuteronomy 7:8–10 and Psalm 145.

2. Reflect on God's faithfulness to *you* in the past, and then reflect on how these past experiences allow you to trust him both in the present and in the future?

3. In John 2:1–11 we see that Mary trusted Jesus to help her resolve the problem of a lack of wine (v. 5), and we also see that the disciples believed in him (v. 11). Reflect on how your faith/belief in Jesus could grow this week through understanding the deeper significance of this sign. Do you trust in Jesus for the difficult areas of your life, or are you trying to resolve your problems in your own strength?

Day Two

1. Read 1 John 1:5–10.

2. Just as Jesus took away the shame of this wedding family that would have been totally embarrassed because they did not provide enough wine (John 2:3), he also takes away our shame as he forgives us on a daily basis (1 John 1:9). Have you allowed Jesus to take away your shame? What would your life look like if all shame were taken away?

3. If the wedding family would have had enough money, they certainly would have bought enough wine so that they would not have run out during the wedding banquet. By presenting this gift of wine, Jesus helped a poor family out of a shameful predicament. It seems that one of the emphases of the new covenant is to minister to the poor (see, for example, Luke 4:18–19). How could you help the poor this week—both financially and spiritually?

Day Three

1. Read John 13:1–17.

2. One of the most amazing aspects of this "first sign" is that it was done in a small, insignificant town, Cana. In fact, it is possible that the wedding family was not even aware of what Jesus had done. This shows us that Jesus is a humble servant who cares

for even the most insignificant of people. He meets our needs. How does this help you to understand God's care and concern for you?

3. True service does not demand attention and pride of place. Jesus did not take the place of importance from the bride and groom, though he was the Son of God! Remember, he said that those who do "acts of righteousness" to impress others will have no reward from the Father" (see Matthew 6:1). As you think about your own deeds of service to others, recall a time when you did it for personal recognition as well as a time when you followed Jesus' example of humble service?

Day Four

1. Read Jeremiah 31:10–17 and John 15:11.

2. The idea of "nations" or "peoples" shows up in the texts we've read in Isaiah, Jeremiah, and Amos. Given that we are to be a blessing to the nations, consider possible changes in your church and in your own life that should result from understanding the importance of this worldwide mission.

3. Jeremiah 31:12 says, "They will come and shout for joy on the heights of Zion; they will rejoice in the bounty of the LORD — the grain, the new wine and the oil." Are you experiencing the joy of Christianity that those in the Old Testament looked forward to? Why or why not?

Day Five

1. Read John 2:1 – 11 one more time.

2. Pray through the entire passage verse by verse, allowing the deeper meaning you have discovered to lead you as you pray. Ask the Spirit to continue to remind you of what you have learned and to help you apply these truths to your life.

3. Turn back to the discussion questions from the video teaching (Video Discussion #1, #2, #3). If there are questions that your group did not have time to discuss or questions that you might like to think more about, use this time to review and reflect further.

Knowing the King

Feeding the 5,000/ Walking on the Water (Matthew 14:15–33)

Dr. Michael Wilkins

And when they climbed into the boat, the wind died down. Then those who were in the boat worshiped him, saying, "Truly you are the Son of God."

⌀ Matthew 14:32–33

In the presence of Jesus, fear can be dismissed.

⌀ R. T. France

INTRODUCTION

Video Opener

Scripture Reading: Matthew 14:15–33, followed by a prayer that God will open your heart as you study his Word

Location of the Miracle: The traditional site of the miracle is west of Capernaum, past the traditional site of the Sermon on the Mount, at present-day Tabgha. A mosaic in the church at Tabgha is shown on the previous page.

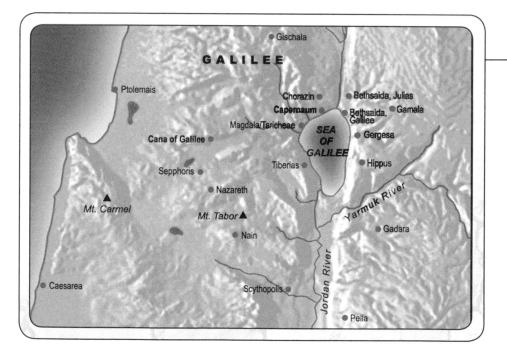

CONNECTING TO THE BIBLE

Jesus had a very specific goal in mind with his announcement, "Repent, for the kingdom of heaven is near." Many who heard him, however, were confused by this message.

Video Teaching #1 Notes

Location of Video Teaching: San Clemente State Beach, California

Jesus the king and his kingdom

> From that time on Jesus began to preach, "Repent, for the kingdom of heaven is near."
>
> Matthew 4:17

Different ideas of what the "kingdom" is

Feeding the five thousand (Matthew 14:15–21)

DID YOU KNOW?

There were five thousand "men," but the total number of people fed in this miracle would have been twenty thousand or more.

The miracle

The crowd's reaction

> After the people saw the miraculous sign that Jesus did, they began to say, "Surely this is the Prophet who is to come into the world." Jesus, knowing that they intended to come and make him king by force, withdrew again to a mountain by himself.
>
> John 6:14–15

According to the Scripture, "They all ate and were satisfied, and the disciples picked up twelve basketfuls of broken pieces that were left over" (Matthew 14:20). This abundance would force the Jewish person to recall the expected abundance in the coming messianic banquet.

Jesus walks on the water (Matthew 14:22–33)

Jesus is alone, in prayer

After he had dismissed them, he went up on a mountainside by himself to pray.

Matthew 14:23

He flees from the temptation to secret prayer, for here is the source of his strength to resist evil.

E. M. Bounds

The disciples are rowing

First-century fishing boat recently found next to the Sea of Galilee

The boat was already a considerable distance from land, buffeted by the waves because the wind was against it.

Matthew 14:24

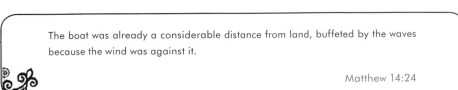

Jesus walks on the water

> During the fourth watch of the night Jesus went out to them, walking on the lake. When the disciples saw him walking on the lake, they were terrified. "It's a ghost," they said, and cried out in fear. But Jesus immediately said to them: "Take courage! It is I. Don't be afraid."
>
> Matthew 14:25–27

VIDEO DISCUSSION #1

1. Looking back at the Bible passage and your video teaching notes, what did you learn that you did not know previously? Consider specifically:

   • Jewish expectations of the messianic king

   • The length of time the disciples were rowing while Jesus prayed

   • The number of people whom Jesus fed

• The geography of the Sea of Galilee

How does this knowledge help you to understand the miracle better?

2. Imagine that you are there on the mountainside receiving the bread from Jesus. Do you think that you would have understood who Jesus was? What parts of the miracle would make you believe that Jesus was indeed the Messiah?

What parts would make you question it?

3. Now imagine that you are there in the boat with the disciples. Keeping in mind that a Jewish person only worships God, do you think that you would have worshiped Jesus after he walked on the water and calmed the storm? Why or why not?

GOING DEEPER

Israel had experienced devastating conquests by foreign nations for centuries. Jerusalem was now occupied by the Romans. As a result, they were looking for a deliverer. Although the crowd didn't understand Jesus' true mission, the time had come for the disciples to step forward.

Video Teaching #2 Notes

The crowd's hope for a Messiah

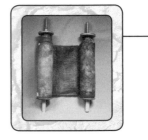

Life in first-century Israel

Awaiting the "Anointed One"

False messianic deliverers

> There was also Simon ... he was bold enough to place the diadem on his head, and having got together a body of men, he was proclaimed king by them in their madness ... but Gratus intercepted him and cut off his head.
>
> Josephus, a Jewish historian

Misunderstanding Jesus

Other messianic misconceptions

> It will happen at that time that the treasure of manna will descend again from the heights, and they will eat it in those years because the consummation of the ages has come.
>
> 2 Baruch 29:8

> As the first redeemer caused manna to descend ... so too the last Redeemer will cause manna to descend.
>
> Midrash Rabbah Ecclesiastes 1:28

The disciples' vision of the true Messiah

The disciples in the storm

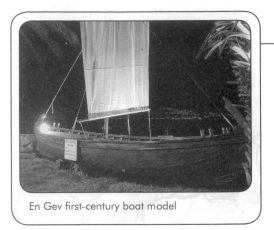
En Gev first-century boat model

Jesus reveals his true identity

The Sea of Galilee with mountains in the background

DID YOU KNOW?

The Sea of Galilee lies 650 feet below sea level and is surrounded by mountains that reach an elevation of 2,000–4,000 feet. The cool Mediterranean air from the west collides with the heated desert air, creating strong winds and frequent storms that swirl over the sea.

Gary Burge

Fear before the presence of God was very common in the Old Testament: Adam is afraid when he hears God's voice in the garden of Eden after sinning; Abraham and his wife Sarah are afraid when God speaks to them; Jacob is afraid after God appears to him in a dream.

"Take courage! It is I. Don't be afraid."

He is not just the Messiah; he is God.

God said to Moses, "I AM WHO I AM. This is what you are to say to the Israelites: 'I AM has sent me to you.'"

Exodus 3:14

Did the disciples understand who Jesus was?

Jesus is worshiped

Then those who were in the boat worshiped him, saying, "Truly you are the Son of God."

Matthew 14:33

VIDEO DISCUSSION #2

1. Did you know before this video teaching that there were varied messianic expectations in the first century? Does that help you to understand the Jewish peoples' confusion over the identity of Jesus? Why or why not?

2. When Jesus "brought manna in the spring," some concluded that he must be the Messiah. Why do you think that he did not just tell the crowd that he was the Messiah? What would the people have thought if he had said this? What problems might it have caused for him?

3. What was it about the events of the miracle of Jesus walking on the water that caused the disciples to begin to understand his identity?

CONNECTING THE BIBLE TO LIFE

Just as the disciples were growing in their understanding of the person of Jesus, it is vitally important for us to develop a clear vision of Jesus so that we can face our storms in life.

Video Teaching #3 Notes

The disciples' limited understanding of Jesus

> Then those who were in the boat worshiped him, saying, "Truly you are the Son of God."
>
> Matthew 14:33
>
> ---
>
> **Peter:** You are the Christ, the Son of the living God.
>
> Matthew 16:16
>
> ---
>
> **Transfiguration:** "This is my Son, whom I love; with him I am well pleased. Listen to him!"
>
> Matthew 17:5

Our understanding of Jesus

Our fragmented images of Jesus

A more complete image of Jesus

Understanding and worshiping Jesus

> Then he got up and rebuked the winds and the waves, and it was completely calm. The men were *amazed* and asked, "What kind of man is this?"
>
> Matthew 8:26–27
>
> ---
>
> Then those who were in the boat *worshiped* him, saying, "Truly you are the Son of God."
>
> Matthew 14:33

Michelle's surfing experience

Looking to the real Jesus in the midst of the storms of life

I had never seen Jesus as I saw him then. I had seen him as powerful. I had seen him as wise. I had witnessed his authority and marveled at his abilities. But what I witnessed last night I know I'll never forget.

I saw God. The God who can't sit still when the storm is too strong. The God who lets me get frightened enough to need him and then comes close enough for me to see him. The God who uses my storms as his path to come to me.

I saw God. It took a storm for me to see him. But I saw him. And I'll never be the same.

Max Lucado

VIDEO DISCUSSION #3

1. We all start out with a level of ineffective faith like Peter, but it grows as Jesus shows himself faithful to us over time. Reflect back over your process of understanding Jesus' true identity from conversion to the present. What events took place that helped you to understand Jesus better? What people helped explain him to you?

2. What advice would you give a new believer who has just started on the path of trying to understand Jesus' true identity?

3. When the crowd wanted to make Jesus king after feeding the five thousand, Jesus went away to pray (Matthew 14:23). Why do you think he sent the disciples away?

MAKING DEEPER CONNECTIONS IN YOUR OWN LIFE

Personal reflection studies to do on your own

Day One

1. Read Mark 6:30–52, noting the similarities to and differences from Matthew 14:15–33.

2. While the disciples were struggling and rowing in the boat for nine hours, Jesus was up in the mountains alongside the Sea of Galilee praying (Matthew 14:22–24). From that vantage point, do you think that he knew that a strong wind was blowing on the sea and that the disciples were struggling? If so, why do you think that he waited nine hours before going to them?

3. Do you think that the disciples were in the will of God as they struggled at sea? Reread Matthew 14:22. Is it possible to be in the will of God and experience suffering?

Day Two

1. Read Luke 9:10–17, noting the similarities to and differences from Matthew 14:15–33.

2. When the crowd wanted to make Jesus king after he fed the five thousand, Jesus went away to pray (John 6:14–15; Matthew 14:23). Why do you think he did this? For what do you think he was praying? What is your normal response when difficult times come?

3. These two incidents also show us that Jesus understood that he and his disciples needed to rest (Mark 6:31). In our culture, the pace of life is so fast that some of us feel guilty when we rest. Jesus, though, took time out to rest and to pray. Reflect and ask God if you are too busy to spend necessary time with him. What good things are you missing because of your busyness?

Day Three

1. Read John 6:1–24 (and verses 25–71 if you have time), noting the similarities to and differences from Matthew 14:15–33.

2. Just as the Jews in Jesus' day had their expectation of who Jesus the Messiah/King should be, we today have our own expectations. What misconceptions do people have today that keep them from accepting Jesus as their Messiah? Is there anything that the church could do to help people understand his true identity?

3. While we often criticize Peter for his lack of faith because he started to sink, he *did* walk on water for a short time— something that most of us have not done (Matthew 14:28–31)! What does the incident teach us about Peter's faith and his developing understanding of who Jesus is? What can we learn from him?

Day Four

1. Read Matthew 6:19–21.

2. We can easily forget the fact that Jesus met the physical needs of the crowd when he performed this miracle of feeding the five thousand (Matthew 14:15–21). Do our ministries today meet the physical needs of people? What about their spiritual needs?

3. Just like Jesus' disciples, we today usually have the resources in our hands (see John 6:9) to help others. Reflect on what resources you and your Christian community presently have that Jesus could use to meet the needs of those around you.

Day Five

1. Read Matthew 14:15–33 one more time.

2. Pray through the entire passage verse by verse, allowing the deeper meaning that you have discovered to lead you as you pray. Ask the Spirit to continue to remind you of what you have learned and to help you apply these truths to your life.

3. Turn back to the discussion questions from the video teaching (Video Discussion #1, #2, #3). If there are questions that your group did not have time to discuss or questions that you might like to think more about, use this time to review and reflect further.

SESSION 4

A Faith-full Outsider

A Canaanite Woman
(Matthew 15:21–28)

Dr. Ben Witherington III

"Woman, you have great faith! Your request is granted." And her daughter was healed from that very hour.

Matthew 15:28

No one else receives from Jesus the accolade *Great is your faith!*

R. T. France

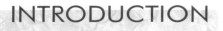
INTRODUCTION

Video Opener

Scripture Reading: Matthew 15:21–28, followed by a prayer that God will open your heart as you study his Word

Location of Miracle: In the region of Tyre and Sidon

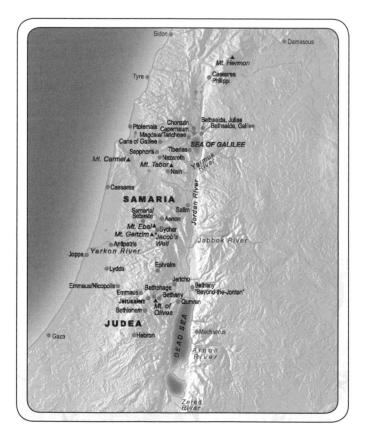

CONNECTING TO THE BIBLE

There is a stark contrast between the "great faith" of the Canaanite woman and the disciples' lack of faith.

Video Teaching #1 Notes

Location of Video Teaching: Old North Church, Boston, Massachusetts

Two troubling aspects in this story

Jesus has gone to Tyre and Sidon

> The term "Canaanite" has inevitable Old Testament associations with the pagan inhabitants of Palestine displaced by the Jews and thus contrasts the woman all the more with the people of God.
>
> Donald Hagner

Conclusion of the story: "great faith"

"Woman, you have great faith!"

Matthew 15:28

A temple dedicated to Eshmun, a god of healing, was located three miles northwest of Sidon. The Canaanite woman instead comes to Jesus for healing her daughter.

Michael Wilkins

Is Jesus being ethnocentric?

Jesus did not answer a word. So his disciples came to him and urged him, "Send her away, for she keeps crying out after us." He answered, "I was sent only to the lost sheep of Israel."

Matthew 15:23–24

The contrast between the disciples' lack of faith and non-Jewish faith

Jewish Disciples: "You of little faith."

Matthew 6:30; 8:26; 14:31; 16:8; see also 17:20

Centurion: Jesus said to the centurion, "Go! It will be done just as you believed it would [according to your faith]."

Matthew 8:13

Canaanite: "Woman, you have great faith!"

Matthew 15:28

The Canaanite woman's persistence

"First let the children eat all they want."

Mark 7:27

—————————————————— ◉ ——————————————————

"It is not right to take the children's bread and toss it to their dogs."

Matthew 15:26

DID YOU KNOW?

"Crying out" in Matthew 15:22 is an imperfect tense in the Greek, suggesting a continuing action: "she kept on crying out to Jesus."

Son of David

Her calling Jesus "Son of David" shows some recognition of Jesus as the Messiah who would heal the people.

D. A. Carson

Jesus' healings and his teaching

The focus here is not on the healing but on the Gentile woman who makes the request.

Donald Hagner

VIDEO DISCUSSION #1

1. Looking back at the Bible passage and your video teaching notes, what did you learn that you did not know previously? Consider specifically:

   • Why Jesus went to Tyre and Sidon (see Mark 7:24)

   • Ethnocentricity of the disciples

   • Contrast of faith between the disciples and non-Jews in Matthew's gospel

   • Difference between healing and teaching in Jesus' ministry

   How does this knowledge help you to understand the miracle better?

2. Why do you think that Jesus initially did not answer the woman and the disciples wanted to send her away (Matthew 15:23)? Why do you think that the disciples could have been ethnocentric, thinking that their race was superior to others (see Deuteronomy 7:6)? Why did Jesus finally answer her?

GOING DEEPER

The Jewish expectation was that the Messiah would come to Israel and bless her. This blessing, though, would overflow to the Gentiles. Many Jewish people expected a mass conversion of Gentiles to Judaism when the Messiah came.

Video Teaching #2 Notes

"Son of David" and exorcisms

> Now the wisdom which God had bestowed on Solomon was so great ... God also enabled him to learn that skill which expels demons.... The manner of the cure was this: He put a ring that had a Foot of one of those sorts mentioned by Solomon to the nostrils of the demoniac, after which he drew out the demon through his nostrils.
>
> Josephus, Jewish historian

Exorcisms and Jewish cleanliness

Jesus' ministry focus: the Jewish people

"I was sent only to the lost sheep of Israel.... It is not right to take the children's bread and toss it to their dogs." "Yes, Lord," she said, "but even the dogs eat the crumbs that fall from their masters' table."

Matthew 15:24, 26–27

The "bread of the children" is a symbol of the messianic fulfillment promised to Israel and now being fulfilled.

John Nolland

Exorcisms: proof of the kingdom of God

"But if I drive out demons by the Spirit of God, then the kingdom of God has come upon you."

Matthew 12:28

Jesus and Gentiles/the nations

"All peoples on earth will be blessed through you."

Genesis 12:3

"I say to you that many will come from the east and the west, and will take their places at the feast with Abraham, Isaac and Jacob in the kingdom of heaven."

Matthew 8:11

The faith of the centurion and the Canaanite woman are exceptions in the ministry of Jesus, which is to bring blessing to humankind universally.

John Nolland

VIDEO DISCUSSION #2

1. Jesus showed great love and compassion in granting the Canaanite woman's request even though it was outside of his main mission to Israel (Matthew 15:24). Imagine what this would have meant to the woman. Have you experienced the love and compassion of Jesus in your life? Share your experience of Jesus' love and compassion with the group.

2. It is interesting that this Canaanite woman came to Jesus, the *Jewish* Messiah, to heal her daughter. How would she have known about him? Why didn't she go to the local temple for healing? Now consider how people today who are outside of our churches know about Jesus. What would cause them to come? What would keep them away?

CONNECTING THE BIBLE TO LIFE

The boldness of the Canaanite woman allows her to be blessed by Jesus.

Video Teaching #3 Notes

Boldness within a situation of having no rights

Paul Revere

Samuel Adams

"So if the Son sets you free, you will be free indeed."

John 8:36

The Canaanite woman

Jesus is the central figure of the story

The Jews universally assumed that eschatological fulfillment belonged to Israel in an exclusive sense, but that the overflow of the abundant eschatological blessing of God would be made available to "righteous" Gentiles.

John Nolland

Jesus is willing to reach out to those who are beyond the pale so that the least, the last, and the lost might become the first, the most, and the found.

Ben Witherington III

VIDEO DISCUSSION #3

1. Ben Witherington said that the Canaanite woman was "not going to leave Jesus without a blessing, without her daughter being set free." She understood that Jesus came to set us free from bondage, so she kept on "crying out" to Jesus to have "mercy" on her (Matthew 15:22). Do you have the kind of "great faith" (15:28) that keeps on crying out to Jesus for not only your own release from bondage but for that of others you know? For what are you crying out to Jesus these days?

2. The exorcism, the bringing of the messianic bread (Matthew 15:26), and his great compassion in this miracle teach us a lot about who Jesus is. Do you think that those in the church today fully understand who Jesus is? Why or why not?

   What could help us to understand him better? Is it just a matter of intellectual knowledge, or is something more involved?

   What difference does it make when we have a fuller understanding of who Jesus is?

MAKING DEEPER CONNECTIONS IN YOUR OWN LIFE

Personal reflection studies to do on your own

Day One

1. Read Matthew 8:5–13.

2. The Canaanite woman had "great faith" (Matthew 15:28), while Jesus' disciples still did not fully understand his mission. How is it possible to walk with Jesus closely as the disciples did and still not have "great faith" in him? If this has been your experience, describe it.

3. Even though a temple dedicated to Eshmun, a god of healing, was located only three miles northwest of Sidon, the Canaanite woman went to Jesus to heal her daughter. She realized that Jesus was the one who could help her. Do you go to Jesus for help, even when there are other options in our world today? If so, explain.

Day Two

1. Read Isaiah 2:1–3; 25:6–9; 42:6–9.

2. God is faithful. In fulfillment of these Old Testament prophecies and many others, Jesus was sent to Israel first and foremost, and the blessings spilled over to the Gentile nations. God has not changed. We can still trust him to deliver on his promises. Spend some time thinking about (and maybe journaling) the promises that God has given to you. Do you still believe his promises?

3. Just like the Jews had to wait for hundreds of years for the fulfillment of the promises to them, we have now waited two thousand years for the second coming of Christ. This text in Isaiah reminds us to be patient and trust God that all of the biblical promises to us will be fulfilled. In the meantime, Jesus calls us to watch and pray (Matthew 26:41) and to be prepared because he will return like a thief in the night (24:42–44). What are you doing on earth to prepare yourself for his second coming?

Day Three

1. Read Romans 12:1–2.

2. The Canaanite woman accepted God's plan of sending Jesus first to Israel (Matthew 15:27). Rather than fighting it, she asked to be considered within it. Do we fight God's plan when it seems

contrary to what we want? Or do we believe that God's plan is better than ours and submit to his "good, pleasing and perfect will" (Romans 12:2)?

3. Matthew 15:24 reminds us that Jesus did not waver from the task that God sent him to do, instead modeling perseverance in mission and faithfulness to his Master. Likewise we ought to single-mindedly pursue the mission that God has given us without wavering from it. What is the "mission" that God has given you? Are you remaining faithful to his calling in your life?

Day Four

1. Read Matthew 15:1–20.

2. The preceding context in Matthew 15:1–20 shows us that it is one's heart that defiles a person, not something on the outside. Despite being ceremonially unclean in every way, the Canaanite woman came to Jesus in faith. This should remind us that we must continually come to Jesus, asking him to change our hearts and move us toward greater faith in him. Spend some time praying that God would change you from the inside out into a clean vessel for his use. Write down any insights from your prayer time.

3. The fact that this woman is a Canaanite reminds us that God shows absolutely no partiality—anyone is welcome to come to him for forgiveness, especially now that we live after the Great Commission (Matthew 28:18–20). How might you more effectively look outside your "circle" to those who need to hear the good news?

Day Five

1. Read Matthew 15:21–28 one more time.

2. Pray through the entire passage verse by verse, allowing the deeper meaning you have discovered to lead you as you pray. Ask the Spirit to continue to remind you of what you have learned and to help you apply these truths to your life.

3. Turn back to the discussion questions from the video teaching (Video Discussion #1, #2, #3). If there are questions that your group did not have time to discuss or questions that you might like to think more about, use this time to review and reflect further.

Fruitless Lives

The Cursing of the Fig Tree (Mark 11:12–21)

Dr. David Garland

Peter remembered and said to Jesus, "Rabbi, look! The fig tree you cursed has withered!"

⌐ Mark 11:21

The fig tree in leaf gave promise of fruit but produced none.

⌐ Craig Blomberg

INTRODUCTION

Video Opener

Scripture Reading: Mark 11:12–21, followed by a prayer that God will open your heart as you study his Word

Location of the Miracle: The cursing of the fig tree takes place as Jesus walked from Bethany to Jerusalem

CONNECTING TO THE BIBLE

This story of Jesus' outrage at a fruitless fig tree is puzzling and quite strange. Why does Jesus vent his anger on this innocent tree? He could have used his power to force a crop.

Video Teaching #1 Notes

Location of Video Teaching: Mountaintop, Colorado Rockies

Jesus curses a fig tree

> "May no one ever eat fruit from you again."
>
> Mark 11:14

The disciples see the withered tree

> In the morning, as they went along, they saw the fig tree withered from the roots. Peter remembered and said to Jesus, "Rabbi, look! The fig tree you cursed has withered!"
>
> Mark 11:20–21

The interlude: Jesus goes to the temple

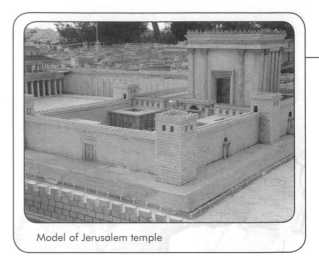

Model of Jerusalem temple

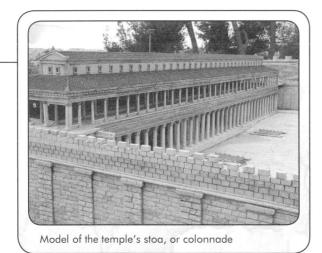

Model of the temple's stoa, or colonnade

Jesus was not surprised by the commercial activity in the temple

The animals for sacrifice

The money changers

> Jesus entered the temple area and began driving out those who were buying and selling there.
>
> Mark 11:15

Silver shekel and half shekel

DID YOU KNOW?

The Tyrian shekel was the closest available currency to the Hebrew shekel commanded in Exodus 30:13–16: it was made of pure metal and did not have any images.

James Edwards

The vessels

[He] would not allow anyone to carry *merchandise* through the temple courts.

Mark 11:16

—————————————————— ◎ ——————————————————

Come out from it and be pure, you who carry the *vessels* of the LORD.

Isaiah 52:11

Models of lampstand (left) and oil holder for the tabernacle (right)

Jesus was not trying to reform the temple

"Do you see all these great buildings?" replied Jesus. "Not one stone here will be left on another; every one will be thrown down."

Mark 13:2

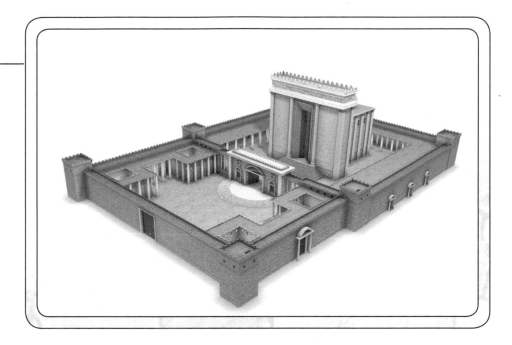

What *was* Jesus doing in the temple?

Jesus' predicted judgment on the temple will come to pass as surely as his prediction of the withering of the fig tree.

W. W. Wessel

VIDEO DISCUSSION #1

1. Looking back at the Bible passage and your video teaching, what did you learn that you did not know previously? Consider specifically:

   • The temple

   • The animals

   • The coins or the money changers

   • The Court of the Gentiles

   How does this knowledge help you to understand the miracle better?

2. Why do you think David Garland has spoken at length about the incident in the temple instead of the cursing of the fig tree? Why do you think that Jesus cast out the animals and the money changers from the temple? What do you think is the relationship between what happened in the temple (Mark 11:15–17) and the cursing of the fig tree (11:12–14, 20–21)?

GOING DEEPER

The cursing of the fig tree wraps around the story of Jesus in the temple. They share a similar point, so they should be read together.

Video Teaching #2 Notes

Cleansing or cursing?

> Cursing the fig tree is an acted parable related to cleansing the temple and conveying a message about Israel.
>
> D. A. Carson

Fig tree fruit

Fig trees: a symbol for the spiritual condition of the people of Israel

> What misery is mine! I am like one who gathers summer fruit at the gleaning of the vineyard; there is no cluster of grapes to eat, none of the early figs that I crave.
>
> Micah 7:1

> When I found Israel, it was like finding grapes in the desert; when I saw your fathers, it was like seeing the early fruit on the fig tree.
>
> Hosea 9:10

The magnificence of the temple buildings

> Being covered on all sides with massive plates of gold, the sun was no sooner up than it radiated so fiery a flash that persons straining to look at it were compelled to avert their eyes, as from the solar rays.
>
> Josephus, Jewish historian

Out of "season"

> "The time has come," he said. "The kingdom of God is near."
>
> Mark 1:15

"Time" has run out for fruitless temples

When he reached it, he found nothing but leaves, because it was not the season for figs. Then he said to the tree, "May no one ever eat fruit from you again."

Mark 11:13–14

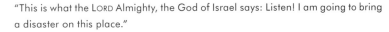

What happened to the fig tree is going to happen to this temple

"This is what the Lord Almighty, the God of Israel says: Listen! I am going to bring a disaster on this place."

Jeremiah 19:3 (see vv. 1–15)

Unless Israel repents, like the fig tree it will perish.

Craig Blomberg

Jerusalem temple ruins

VIDEO DISCUSSION #2

1. David Garland says, "Actions speak louder than words, but not always so clearly." What do you think Jesus' actions said both in the temple incident (Mark 11:15–17) and in the cursing of the fig tree (11:12–14, 20–21)? Why do you think that Jesus did these things?

2. What kind of "fruit" (Mark 11:13–14) do you think Jesus was looking for in the Jewish people?

3. Jesus interpreted his actions in the temple by quoting Isaiah 56:7: "My house will be called a house of prayer for all nations." God did not plan for the temple to become a national shrine for Israel. The context of Isaiah 56:1–8 contains God's promise of blessing for *all* who might think they are excluded from God's salvation: the foreigner (v. 3), the eunuch (vv. 3–4), and the outcasts of Israel (v. 8).

   • How would you feel as a Gentile if you were allowed to enter the temple complex but were barred from entering the sanctuary (see Acts 21:27–32)?

   • Have you ever been forbidden from participating in an activity or entering a place because of your skin color/gender/nationality? If so, describe.

CONNECTING THE BIBLE TO LIFE

The cursing of the fig tree is a dramatic illustration of what is going to happen to the temple. The sacrifices are going to come to an end because God intended that they would be replaced by one sacrifice, Jesus, the Son of God.

Video Teaching #3 Notes

The shift from the temple to Jesus

The curtain of the temple was torn in two from top to bottom.

Mark 15:38

Jesus himself replaces the temple as the center of true worship of God.

Ben Witherington III

"My house will be called a house of prayer for all nations."
(Isaiah 56:7)

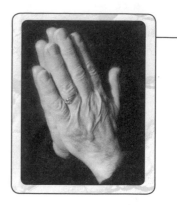

Application today:

The temple was meant to be a house of prayer, but they had made it "a
nationalistic stronghold."

D. A. Carson

"You are making it a 'den of robbers.' " (Matthew 21:13)

"Will you steal and murder, commit adultery and perjury, burn incense to Baal and follow other gods you have not known, and then come and stand before me in this house, which bears my Name, and say, 'We are safe'—safe to do all these detestable things? Has this house, which bears my Name, become a den of robbers to you? But I have been watching! declares the LORD. Go now to the place in Shiloh where I first made a dwelling for my Name, and see what I did to it because of the wickedness of my people Israel."

Jeremiah 7:9–12

The destroyed temple in Shiloh

Application today:

Those who profess to be God's people but live unfruitful lives are warned.

Leon Morris

When he comes, what will he find? Will he find fruit or just leaves? And will he pronounce judgment upon us?

David Garland

VIDEO DISCUSSION #3

1. Though it is true that we have forgiveness of sins through the death of Jesus, and that we no longer need to go to a temple to offer sacrifice, it does not mean that we Christians may presume upon God's forgiveness. God's call to holiness now extends to us (1 Peter 1:15–16). Besides gossip and greed, what other sins do you think we overlook in today's church?

2. What do you think would happen in our personal lives, in our churches, in our neighborhoods, and even in our country if we began to live holy lives and took seriously God's call to eliminate sin from our lives?

3. Like the Jewish people in the first century, how do we sometimes erect barriers in our churches and our individual lives that keep people away from God and the message of his forgiving love through Jesus? What could we do to make our churches and ourselves more inviting to outsiders, while also maintaining the call to holiness?

MAKING DEEPER CONNECTIONS IN YOUR OWN LIFE

Personal reflection studies to do on your own

Day One

1. Read Mark 11:15–17 along with the Old Testament quotation and its context in Jeremiah 7:1–20.

2. In Jeremiah's day, God was gravely concerned about many actions of the Jewish people. He told them to "deal with each other justly … do not oppress the alien, the fatherless or the widow" (Jeremiah 7:5–6) and do not "steal and murder, commit adultery and perjury … and follow other gods" (v. 9). Ask God's Spirit to reveal to you actions or thought patterns in your life that might be displeasing to him. Ask him to forgive you and to cleanse you from all unrighteousness (1 John 1:9).

3. What fruit can you point to in your life today that you struggled to produce or that was not there five years ago? How is your life growing in Christ (2 Peter 1:8)?

Day Two

1. Read Matthew 21:12–20, noting the similarities to and differences from Mark 11:12–21.

2. In Jeremiah 7:16, God told the prophet "do not pray for this people ... for I will not listen." Why do you think God said that? Do you think that there is a point at which God gives us over to our sinful desires (see Romans 1:21–32, especially v. 24)?

3. When we meet up with people who have no fruit, should we "curse" or "judge" them or try to reach them with the good news of the gospel, even when they continue to reject the message? Should we ever give up? Why or why not?

Day Three

1. Read Luke 19:45–48, noting the similarities to and differences from Mark 11:12–21.

2. Many people say that they will repent of their sins later in life after they have "had their fun." What could the lesson of the fig tree in Mark 11:13–14 teach these people?

3. Jesus stood up before wickedness and condemned it (Mark 11:15–17). Reflect on what Christians today, in our politically correct climate, do when we are surrounded by wickedness. How should we respond to wickedness?

Day Four

1. Read John 2:13–25, noting the similarities to and differences from Mark 11:12–21.

2. Some people have attended church all their lives. They have the outward look of fruitfulness, but inside there is a lack of fruit. Reflect on your life and that of your church. How can we seek God's help to ensure that true Christian fruit is found in our lives?

3. Jeremiah took a long-necked jug, smashed it in front of the elders and priests, and in essence said, "This is what is going to happen to you" (Jeremiah 19:1–15). In the Mark passage Jesus also acted like a prophet when he cursed the fig tree and

overturned the tables in the temple. If Jesus were to show up in your life today, what action might he take to symbolically show what he sees in your life? Would it be a positive or a negative action?

Day Five

1. Read Mark 11:12–21 one more time.

2. Pray through the entire passage verse by verse, allowing the deeper meaning you have discovered to lead you as you pray. Ask the Spirit to continue to remind you of what you have learned and to help you apply these truths to your life.

3. Turn back to the discussion questions from the video teaching (Video Discussion #1, #2, #3). If there are questions that your group did not have time to discuss or questions that you might like to think more about, use this time to review and reflect further.

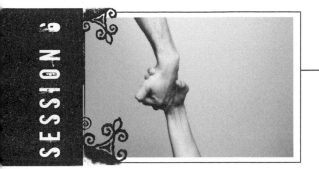

SESSION 6

Grateful Outcasts

Ten Lepers
(Luke 17:11 – 19)

Dr. Mark Strauss

"Were not all ten cleansed? Where are the other nine?"

Luke 17:17

God is not an ogre who hoards his compassion and needs persuading to exercise it.

Darrell Bock

INTRODUCTION

Video Opener

Scripture Reading: Luke 17:11 – 19, followed by a prayer that God will open your heart as you study his Word

Location of Miracle: Along the border of Samaria and Galilee

CONNECTING TO THE BIBLE

The first-century culture in which Jesus lived had many people who lived on the margin of society, such as lepers. They were outsiders looking in, hoping that Jesus would have mercy on them.

Video Teaching #1 Notes

Location of Video Teaching: A park in San Diego, California

People living on the margins

> When anyone has a swelling or a rash or a bright spot on his skin that may become an infectious skin disease, he must be brought to Aaron the priest or to one of his sons who is a priest.
>
> Leviticus 13:2

What is leprosy?

DID YOU KNOW?

Perhaps the closest cultural equivalent to first-century attitudes about leprosy would be current attitudes about bird flu and the fear and quarantine issues that surround it.

On the road to Jerusalem: the gospel to the outcasts

> As the time approached for him to be taken up to heaven, Jesus resolutely set out for Jerusalem.
>
> Luke 9:51

Jesus continues to minister to any who reach out to him. None is turned away.

Darrell Bock

The Samaritan leper: outcast among outcasts

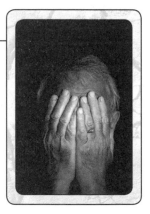

DID YOU KNOW?

The region of Samaria in Old Testament times was inhabited by the ten northern tribes of Israel. Following the death of Solomon, the northern tribes seceded from the tribes of Judah and Benjamin in the south. The southern kingdom became known as Judah, while the northern kingdom was initially known as Israel, until it came to be called Samaria after its capital city.

Craig Evans

Ten lepers ask Jesus for healing

> "Jesus, Master, have pity on us!"
>
> Luke 17:13

Jesus responds

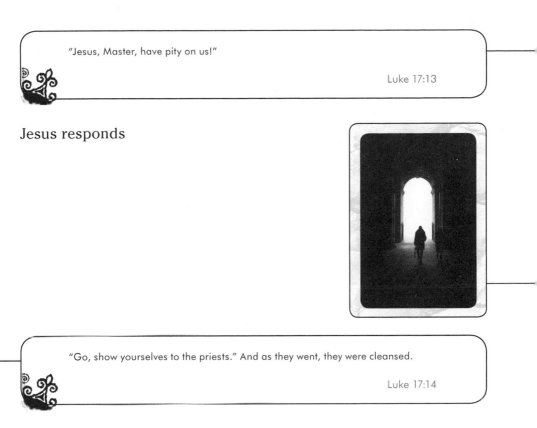

> "Go, show yourselves to the priests." And as they went, they were cleansed.
>
> Luke 17:14

One returns to thank Jesus

> One of them, when he saw he was healed, came back, praising God in a loud voice. He threw himself at Jesus' feet and thanked him—and he was a Samaritan.
>
> Luke 17:15–16

VIDEO DISCUSSION #1

1. Looking back at the Bible passage and your video teaching, what did you learn that you did not know previously? Consider specifically:

   • Leprosy

   • The context of Luke 17

   • The Samaritan as an outcast of outcasts

   • The need for the lepers to have faith *before* they are healed

   How does this knowledge help you to understand the miracle better?

2. Why do you think that only one of the ten lepers returned to thank Jesus (Luke 17:15)? What do you think is significant about Luke's mentioning that he was a Samaritan (17:16)?

GOING DEEPER

Jesus' Jewish hearers would be delighted to hear that these lepers were healed. But then they would have been shocked to hear that the only one who came back to thank Jesus was a Samaritan.

Video Teaching #2 Notes

Jews and Samaritans in the first century

Ruins of Mount Gerizim temple in Samaria, destroyed by the Jews

God is supposedly speaking, and he says, Two nations my soul detests, and the third is not even a people: Those who live in Seir [Edom], and the Philistines, and the foolish people that live in Shechem [Samaria].

Sirach 50:25–26

The hated Samaritan returns to thank Jesus

> [He] came back, praising God in a loud voice.
>
> Luke 17:15

He does not go to the temple to offer sacrifice to God for his cleansing, but returns to Jesus. He recognizes that the restorative power of God is in Jesus.

Joel Green

Only here in all the New Testament are such thanks directed to Jesus. Elsewhere they are directed to God.

Robert Stein

Why didn't the other nine return? Reciprocity in first-century Israel

The spiritual significance of healing

"Rise and go; your faith has made you well."

Luke 17:19

———————————————— ◎ ————————————————

Then will the eyes of the blind be opened and the ears of the deaf unstopped. Then will the lame leap like a deer, and the mute tongue shout for joy.

Isaiah 35:5–6

———————————————— ◎ ————————————————

"Which is easier: to say, 'Your sins are forgiven,' or to say, 'Get up and walk'? But that you may know that the Son of Man has authority on earth to forgive sins...." He said to the paralyzed man, "I tell you, get up, take your mat and go home."

Luke 5:23–24

Jesus is here to provide healing: physical and spiritual

It was well with his soul and with his body.

Leon Morris

VIDEO DISCUSSION #2

1. Given this background of division between the Jews and the Samaritans, if you were a Jew in the first century, what would you think upon hearing that only a *Samaritan* leper returned to thank Jesus for the healing miracle?

2. Mark Strauss said that "Jesus was here to change the course of human history; to provide salvation through the forgiveness of sins, to reverse the results of the fall; to bring true restoration to creation." Do you think that the Christian community in your area has this same mission? Why or why not?

   What is the Christian community in your area doing well and what should they be doing differently?

CONNECTING THE BIBLE TO LIFE

The lepers represent us. We are all sinners in need of grace. As God has offered us his free grace, he calls us to offer it to others.

Video Teaching #3 Notes

A grateful heart

Give thanks in all circumstances.

1 Thessalonians 5:18

Always giving thanks to God the Father for everything.

Ephesians 5:20

Every good and perfect gift is from above, coming down from the Father.

James 1:17

Step out in faith and obedience

Offer his grace to all people everywhere

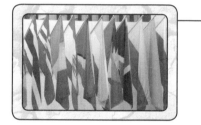

VIDEO DISCUSSION #3

1. What do you do to cultivate a grateful heart? Have you ever tried to look for the blessings that surround you every day?

2. Mark Strauss said, "As we respond in faith, we are 'healed' as the lepers were healed. God says, 'Walk with me on this journey and you will experience fulfillment and joy in the midst of obedience.'" Do you find it difficult to go against the culture's stream and to trust God at his word, walking in faith and obedience in such things as marital fidelity (Ephesians 5:31, 33), material possessions (Matthew 6:19), contentedness (Philippians 4:11), and benevolence (1 John 3:17)? Explain.

3. Despite a long history of differences between Samaritans and Jews, in this miracle Jesus healed a Samaritan—both physically and spiritually. Compare first-century cultural racism to that in our own day. Do you think the church in your community offers the good news of salvation to *all* people, regardless of race or background? Explain.

MAKING DEEPER CONNECTIONS IN YOUR OWN LIFE

Personal reflection studies to do on your own

Day One

1. Read John 4:1–42.

2. Some people have a view of God as a "bad cop" who withholds his compassion from people and is always ready to punish. Reflect on the Luke 17 passage which shows that God has compassion on all ten lepers (vv. 14, 17) even though only one of them responds to this compassion (vv. 15–16). How has God been compassionate to you? Spend some time in prayer thanking him for the compassion that he has shown to you.

3. As Mark Strauss said, how many times in our daily lives do we receive the blessings of God but fail to thank him? What are you thankful for? Take some time right now to thank God for the various blessings that he has brought into your life. Ask him to help you to have a grateful heart today, whatever your circumstances (1 Thessalonians 5:18).

Day Two

1. Read Luke 10:25–37.

2. The healing of the lepers reminds us that faith does not wait, but steps out, trusting God to do what is needed. How long has it been since you "stepped out in faith"? Is God showing you an area in your life in which you could step out in faith? If so, what is it?

3. Ten lepers experienced the compassion and grace of God, yet only one had "faith" that made him well (Luke 17:17–19). Reflect on how people in your community experience the goodness of God on so many levels, yet they do not have faith in him and thus do not receive salvation. What holds them back? What could you do to help them see and respond to the good things that God has done for them?

Day Three

1. Read Psalm 22:22–27.

2. While we can give thanks to God at any time, it is during "worship" or "praise" times in a church service that we can corporately give thanks to God. Do you find your church's worship time to be a good opportunity for you to praise and thank God, or are you distracted by other things during that time? What could you do to make it more of a praise experience?

3. Just as the ten lepers banded together to have community, it is important for us Christians to have community. In contrast to many other places in the world, a majority of Westerners tend to see Christianity more as an individual experience and less a community one. What could you do to build more community into your life?

Day Four

1. Read James 2:1–11.

2. Just as the leper was an outcast in his society, in many ways the poor are outcasts in our society today. James 2:1–11 instructs us not to show favoritism to the rich person over the poor. Are you reaching out to the poor in your area? Is your church? What else could you do to help the poor both physically and spiritually?

3. Who are the other outcasts in your community? How are you reaching out to them with the compassion and grace of God? Have any of them responded in faith? What do you think holds them back from responding to God?

Day Five

1. Read Luke 17:11–19 one more time.

2. Pray through the entire passage verse by verse, allowing the deeper meaning that you have discovered to lead you as you pray. Ask the Spirit to continue to remind you of what you have learned and to help you apply these truths to your life.

3. Turn back to the discussion questions from the video teaching (Video Discussion #1, #2, #3). If there are questions that your group did not have time to discuss or questions that you might like to think more about, use this time to review and reflect further.

Source Acknowledgments

(These are noted in order of appearance for each session. When quoted from a commentary, full source information can be found in "Books for Further Reading" beginning on page 131.)

Session One

Page 11: Edwards, *Mark*, 164.
Page 13: Guelich, *Mark*, 295.
Page 14: Lane, *Mark*, 192.
Page 18: Pliny the Elder, *Natural History*, Book 28.23.78–80, 7.65.
Page 19: Garland, *Mark*, 219.
Page 20: Fackler, *Mark*, 144.
Page 20: Morris, *Matthew*, 230.
Page 22: Wessel, *Matthew, Mark, Luke*, 662.
Page 23: France, *Mark*, 238.
Page 23: Lane, *Mark*, 193.
Page 23: Garland, *Mark*, 225.

Session Two

Page 29: Morris, *John*, 3.
Page 30: Carson, *John*, 168.
Page 32: Beasley-Murray, *John*, 35.
Page 33: Carson, *John*, 169.
Page 37: Beasley-Murray, *John*, 36.
Page 38: Keener, *Bible Background Commentary*, 268.
Page 40: Blomberg, *Contagious Holiness*, Downers Grove, Ill: InterVarsity Press, 2005, 106.
Page 40: Witherington III, *Mark*, 80.

Session Three

Page 51: France, *Matthew*, 239.

Page 55: E. M. Bounds, *"The Reality of Prayer,"* in *The Classic Collection on Prayer*, 342.
Page 58: Josephus, *Antiquities* 17.273–277. Cf. 20.97–98; 168–171; *Jewish War* 2.261–279.
Page 60: Burge, *John*, 192.
Page 65: Max Lucado, *In the Eye of the Storm*, Dallas: Word, 1991, 182.

Session Four

Page 71: France, *Matthew*, 247.
Page 73: Hagner, *Matthew*, 441.
Page 74: Wilkins, *Matthew*, 539.
Page 76: Carson, *Matthew*, 354.
Page 76: Hagner, *Matthew*, 439.
Page 78: Josephus, *Antiquities*, 8, 2, 5.
Page 79: Nolland, *Matthew*, 443.
Page 80: Ibid.
Page 83: Ibid., 442.

Session Five

Page 89: Blomberg, *Matthew*, 530.
Page 93: Edwards, *Mark*, 341.
Page 95: Wessel, *Matthew, Mark, Luke*, 729.
Page 97: Carson, *Matthew, Mark, Luke*, 444.
Page 98: Josephus, *Loeb Classical Library*, 222–223.
Page 99: Blomberg, *Matthew*, 318.
Page 101: Witherington III, *Mark*, 311.
Page 102: Carson, *Matthew, Mark, Luke*, 442.
Page 103: Morris, *Matthew*, 530.

Session Six

Page 109: Bock, *Luke*, 446.
Page 112: Ibid.
Page 112: Evans, *Luke*, 258.
Page 115: Morris, *John*, 227.
Page 116: Green, *Luke*, 621.
Page 116: Stein, *Luke*, 435.
Page 117: Morris, *Luke*, 283.
Page 120: Garland, *Mark*, 227.

Map, Illustration, and Photo Credits

Maps: Mountain High Maps®. Copyright © 1993 Digital Wisdom, Inc.

Todd Bolen: pages 30, 60 (top)

Zev Radovan: pages 32, 58, 93

T. J. Rathbun: pages 19 (bottom), 55, 60 (bottom), 92, 99

Caleb Williams/Mosaic Graphics: page 95

Zondervan Image Archives (Neal Bierling): pages 51, 97, 101, 103, 115

iStockphoto.com: pages 11, 13, 15, 18, 19 (top), 23, 29, 31, 36, 37, 38, 39, 43, 45, 71, 75, 80, 82, 83, 89, 98, 102, 109, 112, 113, 119, 120

Books for Further Reading

Four Gospels

Evans, Craig A., gen ed. *The Bible Knowledge Background Commentary: Matthew–Luke.* Colorado Springs: Victor Books, 2003.

Keener, Craig S. *The IVP Bible Background Commentary: New Testament.* Downers Grove, Ill.: InterVarsity Press, 1993.

Matthew

Barton, Bruce B. *Matthew.* Life Application Bible Commentary. Wheaton, Ill.: Tyndale, 1996.

Blomberg, Craig L. *Matthew.* New American Commentary, vol. 22. Nashville: Broadman, 1992.

Carson, D. A. *Matthew, Mark, Luke.* The Expositor's Bible Commentary, vol. 8. Grand Rapids, Mich.: Zondervan, 1984.

———. *When Jesus Confronts the World: An Exposition of Matthew 8–10.* Grand Rapids, Mich.: Baker, 1987.

Davies, W. D. and Dale C. Allison, Jr. *A Critical and Exegetical Commentary on the Gospel According to Saint Matthew.* The International Critical Commentary. 3 vols. Edinburgh: T. & T. Clark, 1988, 1991, 1997.

France, R. T. *The Gospel According to Matthew: An Introduction and Commentary.* Tyndale New Testament Commentaries, vol. 1. Grand Rapids, Mich.: Eerdmans, 1985.

Green, Michael. *The Message of Matthew: The Kingdom of Heaven.* The Bible Speaks Today Series. Downers Grove, Ill.: InterVarsity Press, 2000.

Guelich, Robert A. *Sermon on the Mount: A Foundation for Understanding.* Waco, Tex.: Word, 1982.

Gundry, Robert. *Matthew: A Commentary on His Handbook for a Mixed Church Under Persecution.* Grand Rapids, Mich.: Eerdmans, 2nd ed. 1994.

Hagner, Donald. *Matthew*. Word Biblical Commentary, vol. 33 a&b. Waco, Tex.: Word, 1993, 1995.

Keener, Craig S. *A Commentary on the Gospel of Matthew*. Grand Rapids, Mich.: Eerdmans, 1999.

Morris, Leon. *The Gospel According to Matthew*. The Pillar New Testament Commentary. Grand Rapids, Mich.: Eerdmans, 1992.

Mounce, Robert H. *Matthew*. New International Biblical Commentary, vol. 1. Peabody, Mass.: Hendrickson, 1991.

Nolland, John. *The Gospel of Matthew: A Commentary on the Greek Text*. The New International Greek Testament Commentary. Grand Rapids, Mich.: Eerdmans, 2005.

Simonetti, Manlio, ed. *Matthew*. Ancient Christian Commentary on Scripture. 2 vols. Downers Grove, Ill.: InterVarsity Press, 2002.

Turner, David and Darrell L. Bock. *Matthew, Mark*. Cornerstone Biblical Commentary. Wheaton, Ill.: Tyndale, 2006.

Wilkins, Michael J. *Matthew*. The NIV Application Commentary. Grand Rapids, Mich.: Zondervan, 2004.

———. *Zondervan Illustrated Bible Backgrounds Commentary*, vol. 1. Grand Rapids, Mich.: Zondervan, 2002.

Mark

Cole, R. Alan. *The Gospel According to Mark*. Tyndale New Testament Commentaries, vol. 2. Grand Rapids, Mich.: Eerdmans, 2002.

Cranfield, C. E. B. *The Gospel According to Saint Mark: An Introduction and Commentary*. Cambridge Greek Testament Commentary. Cambridge, England: Cambridge University Press, 1972.

Edwards, James R. *The Gospel According to Mark*. The Pillar New Testament Commentary. Grand Rapids, Mich.: Eerdmans, 2002.

Evans, Craig. *Mark*. Word Biblical Commentary, vol. 34b. Nashville: Thomas Nelson, 2001.

Fackler, Mark. *Mark*. Life Application Bible Commentary. Wheaton, Ill.: Tyndale, 1994.

France, R. T. *The Gospel of Mark: A Commentary on the Greek Text*. The New International Greek New Testament Commentary. Grand Rapids, Mich.: Eerdmans, 2002.

Garland, David E. *Mark*. The NIV Application Commentary. Grand Rapids, Mich.: Zondervan, 1996.

———. *Zondervan Illustrated Bible Backgrounds Commentary*, vol. 1. Grand Rapids, Mich.: Zondervan, 2002.

Guelich, Robert A. *Mark*. Word Biblical Commentary, vol. 34a. Dallas: Word, 1989.

Gundry, Robert H. *Mark: A Commentary on His Apology for the Cross.* Grand Rapids, Mich.: Eerdmans, 1993.

Lane, William L. *The Gospel According to Mark: The English Text with Introduction, Exposition, and Notes.* The New International Commentary on the New Testament. Grand Rapids, Mich.: Eerdmans, 1974.

Mann, C. S. *Mark: A New Translation with Introduction and Commentary.* Garden City, N.Y.: Doubleday, 1986.

Oden, Thomas C. and Christopher A. Hall, eds. *Mark.* Ancient Christian Commentary on Scripture, vol. 2. Downers Grove, Ill.: InterVarsity Press, 1998.

Taylor, Vincent. *The Gospel According to St. Mark: The Greek Text with Introduction, Notes, and Indexes.* Thornapple Commentaries. Grand Rapids, Mich.: Baker, 2nd ed. 1981.

Wessel, Walter W. *Matthew, Mark, Luke.* The Expositor's Bible Commentary, vol. 8. Grand Rapids, Mich.: Zondervan, 1984.

Witherington, Ben III. *The Gospel of Mark: A Socio-Rhetorical Commentary.* Grand Rapids, Mich.: Eerdmans, 2001.

Luke

Barton, Bruce B., Dave Veerman, and Linda K. Taylor. *Luke.* Life Application Bible Commentary. Wheaton, Ill.: Tyndale, 1997.

Bock, Darrell L. *Luke.* The NIV Application Commentary. Grand Rapids, Mich.: Zondervan, 1996.

Evans, Craig A. *Luke.* New International Biblical Commentary, vol. 3. Peabody, Mass.: Hendrickson, 1990.

Fitzmyer, J. A. *The Gospel According to Luke: Introduction, Translation, and Notes.* Anchor Bible, vol. 28–28a. Garden City, N.Y.: Doubleday, 1981–1985.

Green, Joel B. *The Gospel of Luke.* New International Commentary on the New Testament. Grand Rapids, Mich.: Eerdmans, 1997.

Just, Arther A. Jr., ed. *Luke.* Ancient Christian Commentary on Scripture, vol. 3. Downers Grove, Ill.: InterVarsity Press, 2003.

Liefeld, Walter L. *Matthew, Mark, Luke.* The Expositor's Bible Commentary, vol. 8. Grand Rapids, Mich.: Zondervan, 1984.

Marshall, I. Howard. *Luke: Historian and Theologian.* Grand Rapids, Mich.: Zondervan, 1980.

Morris, Leon. *Luke: An Introduction and Commentary.* Tyndale New Testament Commentaries, vol. 3. Grand Rapids, Mich.: Eerdmans, 1988.

Nolland, John. *Luke.* Word Biblical Commentary, vol. 35a–c. Dallas: Word, 1989–1993.

Stein, Robert H. *Luke.* The New American Commentary, vol. 24. Nashville: Broadman, 1992.

Strauss, Mark L. *Zondervan Illustrated Bible Backgrounds Commentary*, vol. 1. Grand Rapids, Mich.: Zondervan, 2002.

John

Barrett, C. K. *The Gospel According to St. John: An Introduction with Commentary and Notes on the Greek Text.* Philadelphia: Westminster Press, 1978.

Barton, Bruce B. *John.* Life Application Bible Commentary. Wheaton, Ill.: Tyndale, 1993.

Beasley-Murray, George R. *John.* Word Biblical Commentaries, vol. 36. Nashville: Thomas Nelson, 1999.

Brown, Raymond Edward. *The Gospel According to John.* Anchor Bible, vol. 29–29a. Garden City, N.Y.: Doubleday, 1966–1970.

Burge, Gary M. *John.* The NIV Application Commentary. Grand Rapids, Mich.: Zondervan, 2000.

Card, Michael. *The Parable of Joy: Reflections on the Wisdom of the Book of John.* Nashville: Thomas Nelson, 1995.

Carson, D. A. *The Gospel According to John.* The Pillar New Testament Commentary. Grand Rapids, Mich.: Eerdmans, 1991.

Keener, Craig S. *The Gospel of John: A Commentary.* 2 vols. Peabody, Mass.: Hendrickson, 2003.

Köstenberger, Andreas J. *John.* Baker Exegetical Commentary on the New Testament. Grand Rapids, Mich.: Baker, 2004.

———. *Zondervan Illustrated Bible Backgrounds Commentary*, vol. 2. Grand Rapids, Mich.: Zondervan, 2002.

Morris, Leon. *The Gospel According to John.* New International Commentary on the New Testament. Grand Rapids, Mich.: Eerdmans, 1995.

Tasker, R. V. G. *The Gospel According to St. John: An Introduction and Commentary.* Tyndale New Testament Commentaries. Grand Rapids, Mich.: Eerdmans, 1960.

Tenney, Merrill C. *John, Acts.* The Expositor's Bible Commentary, vol. 9. Grand Rapids, Mich.: Zondervan, 1984.

Whitacre, Rodney A. *John.* The IVP New Testament Commentary Series, vol. 4. Downers Grove, Ill.: InterVarsity Press, 1999.

Miracles

Brown, Colin. *Miracles and the Critical Mind.* Grand Rapids: Eerdmans, 1984.

Geivett, R. Douglas and Gary R. Habermas. *In Defense of Miracles: A Comprehensive Case for God's Action in History.* Downers Grove, Ill.: InterVarsity Press, 1997.

Lewis, C. S. *Miracles.* San Francisco: HarperSanFrancisco, 2001.

Twelftree, Graham H. *Jesus the Miracle Worker.* Downers Grove, Ill.: InterVarsity Press, 1999.

Wenham, David and Craig Blomberg, eds. *The Miracles of Jesus.* Sheffield, England: JSOT Press, 1986.

Wilkins, Michael, J. and J. P. Moreland, eds. *Jesus Under Fire.* Grand Rapids, Mich.: Zondervan, 1995.

CHRISTIAN HISTORY MADE EASY

12-Session DVD Study for Individual or Group Use
by Timothy Paul Jones, PhD

Complete *Christian History Made Easy* Study Kit
Contains each of the following items
ISBN: 9781596365254

The DVD
• All 12 DVD sessions, each about 30 minutes • Leader Guide on disc as a printable PDF • Fliers, bulletin inserts, posters & banners as PDFs on disc.
ISBN: 9781596365261

Leader Guide
• Leader Guide gives step-by-step instructions for group hosts or facilitators so you don't have to be the expert.
ISBN: 9781596365278

Participant Guide
• Purchase one for each participant.
• Includes group discussion questions, session outlines, key terms and definitions, Bible study questions, and more.
ISBN: 9781596365285

PowerPoint® Presentation
• Contains more than 300 slides to expand the scope of the teaching ISBN: 9781596363410

Christian History Made Easy Book
• 224 pages, paperback
ISBN: 9781596363281

HOW WE GOT THE BIBLE

DVD Bible Study for Individual or Group Use

Complete *How We Got the Bible* DVD Bible Study Kit

Contains each of the following items
ISBN: 9781628622072

How We Got the Bible DVD Bible Study

• All six DVD sessions • Leader Guide on disc as a printable PDF •
Fliers, bulletin inserts, posters & banners as PDFs on disc
ISBN: 9781628622065

Leader Guide

• Leader Guide gives step-by-step instructions for group hosts or facilitators so you don't have to be the expert.
ISBN: 9781628622089

Participant Guide

• Purchase one for each participant.
• Includes group discussion questions, session outlines, key terms and definitions, Bible study questions, and more.
ISBN: 9781628622126

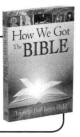

PowerPoint® presentation

• Contains more than 100 slides to expand the scope of the teaching ISBN: 9781890947460

Pamphlet

• Fold-out time line of key events
ISBN: 9781628620825

How We Got the Bible handbook

• Goes into more depth
• Explores the historical background
• 180-page paperback
ISBN: 9781628622164

FEASTS OF THE BIBLE
DVD Bible Study for Individual or Group Use

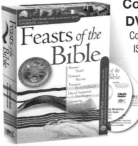

Complete *Feasts of the Bible* DVD Bible Study Kit
Contains each of the following items
ISBN: 9781596364646

Feasts of the Bible DVD Bible Study Leader Pack
• All six DVD-based sessions • Leader Guide on disc as a printable PDF • Fliers, bulletin inserts, posters & banners as PDFs on disc ISBN: 9781596364653

Leader Guide
• Leader Guide gives step-by-step instructions for group hosts or facilitators so you don't have to be the expert
ISBN: 9781596364660

Participant Guide
• Each participant will need a guide
• Guide contains definitions, charts, comparisons, Bible references, discussion questions, and more
ISBN: 9781596364677

Feasts of the Bible PowerPoint® presentation
• Contains more than 100 slides to expand the scope of the teaching ISBN: 9781596361775

Feasts of the Bible pamphlet
• Chart showing each feast, the date, biblical passage, and symbolism fulfilled by Jesus
ISBN: 9781890947583

Messiah in the Feasts of Israel handbook
• Goes into greater depth on all the feasts
• Gives insights into God's redemptive plan, discusses the prophetic purposes of the feasts
• 236-page paperback
ISBN: 9780970261977

We want to hear from you. Please send your comments about this book to us in care of info@hendricksonrose.com. Thank you.

www.hendricksonrose.com